All

Ravindra Kumar, Ph D
(Swami Atmananda)

New Dawn

NEW DAWN
a division of Sterling Publishers (P) Ltd.
L-10, Green Park Ext. New Delhi-110016
Tel : 6198560
E-mail : ghai@nde.vsnl.net.in
www.sterlingpublishers.com

All You Wanted to Know About - Mantra
© 2001, Sterling Publishers Private Limited
ISBN 81 207 2354 6
Reprint 2003

Published by Sterling Publishers Pvt. Ltd., New Delhi-110020.
Lasertypeset by Vikas Compographics, New Delhi-110020.
Printed at Shagun Composer, New Delhi-110029.

Contents

Preface

The use of mantras, for self-realisation and for knowing God, has been made in India since time immemorial. Nevertheless, study and research has shown that mantras were used in different parts of the world, by people of all faiths and traditions, although in a limited way. Mantras used in conjunction with other practices, such as yoga and meditation, have been found to yield quicker results.

In this small book, I endeavour to present the theory and practice of mantras as it has been used at our academy for several years. Nevertheless, I wish to thank the authors whose works I have consulted from time to time. My thanks are also due to William Henry Belk II for discussing various aspects of this book with me. Last but not the least, I thank Jytte Kumar Larsen for providing computing facilities.

Introduction

Aarti, puja, chanting of mantras —
these have been my companions, for
long, under all conditions. When we
chant the 'name of God' we find that
it is a combination of sacred
syllables. These syllables are
different in different faiths and
traditions. For example, Hindus call
such a combination a mantra.
Hence, a mantra might be known by
various names in different parts of
the world. Such a combination of

sacred syllables is believed to have some spiritual meaning, and chanting it leads to a spiritual experience. To understand the meaning and effect of such sacred syllables is the subject matter of this book.

Defining Mantras

Can you recall experiences from everyday life in which calling a person by his name in different ways has different effects? Let me explain using the following example; my youngest uncle, Prabhu Singh would sleep till late in the morning. My grandfather would first try to wake him gently, saying, "Prabhu Singh, get up my son", but my uncle would continue to sleep. Next, my grandfather would call him in a slightly sterner tone:

"Prabhu, it is time for you to get up." My uncle would mutter something but would not get up. Finally, my grandfather would shout in anger: "Prabhua, you donkey, will you get up or should I beat you with a stick?"My uncle, on perceiving the change in the tone, from gentle 'Prabhu' to harsh 'Prabhua', would then make an effort to get out of bed. Hence this example emphasises the fact that the same name 'Prabhu' can affect a person in different ways if the tone and the manner of pronouncing the word are changed.

When the way of pronouncing names affects a human being so much, you can imagine how the entities of the higher realm would be affected when we call them differently. It may be God, or demigods, or a saint or a prophet. Vibrations on higher realms are much finer than the vibrations on earth. The way of pronouncing names has an immense effect, good or bad. If a name is called out correctly and pleasantly with reverence, it attracts the entity being called towards you, and it also attracts power from the universe. If a name is pronounced incorrectly and without any reverence, then it neither attracts the entity from the higher realm, nor does it have any power in it.

A mantra is a set of sacred names or syllables, combined in such a way that it attracts spiritual power like a magnet, or like a lens, passing through which the sunlight converges to a point. Most religions believe that the mantra has the power to create and destroy. For example in Hinduism it was the *shabda* spoken by a Brahman, which created the universe. In Judaism (or

Christianity) we find that everything was created by the *word*. In Islam it is the *kalma-i-ilahi*. Similar names can be found in other faiths and traditions. The *shabda* or *word* or *kalma-i-ilahi* was the first mantra which manifested the spiritual powers of the universe. The practical representation of *shabda* in Hinduism is *Om*, which represents the power of God or God Himself. Most of the other mantras begin with *Om*. There are two representations — *varnatmik* and *dhunatmik*. *Shabda* is varnatmik — theoretical and descriptive; *Om* is dhunatmik

—practical and the cause of manifestation of the spiritual power of the universe.

Man means 'to think' and *tra* means 'to liberate', therefore the literal meaning of mantra is 'thought that liberates'. Mantras, vibrating in ether, were perceived by the evolved souls known as *Rishis* and were brought down by them in a simplified manner. The chanting of a mantra concentrates the spiritual forces within and eventually awakens the *Kundalini* or the dormant serpent power. With this awakening, the dormant centres of the brain are activated and geniuses are born. If the process continues successfully, the Third Eye will open one day, and that would be the opening of the gateway to liberation. As more and more people have been chanting the mantra, for thousands of years, its power has multiplied numerous times and the mantra has become a potential source of power for the user.

The underlying principles of mantra work in a definite sequence. When a mantra is repeatedly chanted in the right style, a stage comes when it acquires a self-generating power, which works like a flywheel, and the mantra is imbibed by the practitioner effortlessly. This is due to the seed (*bija*) within the mantra. When this happens, a link is set up between the practitioner and the deity related to the *bija* of the mantra. The male aspect of God is the 'static potential energy' and the female aspect is the 'creative kinetic energy', called *Shakti*, which is inherent in the mantra. Continued repetition of a mantra, aided by *Shakti*, releases the potency of the mantra and a spiritual awakening is experienced. The deity of the *bija* in the mantra manifests before the practitioner and the practitioner is united with God. This is the real meaning of 'yoga', and the goal of mantra is thus achieved.

There are various aspects of God. A deity represents one particular aspect of God. So it does not matter which deity one follows: the ultimate result is the same, provided one's faith is firm. That way, any one of the *bija* mantras can lead to the goal. However, a mantra which has been repeated numerous times by the practitioner, over the years, becomes a concentrated source of power. Moreover, all the 'liberated souls' or the gurus of the lineage of that mantra, are available to the practitioner for help, on whatever realm they may exist. Such gurus are always looking for disciples who are ready for evolution and who need their guidance and help.

The repetition of the mantra automatically protects the practitioner from the clutches of 'maya' or illusion. This is because of *Shakti*, which is latent in the mantra.

Chanting of Mantras

Although there are several kinds of yoga, beginning from the Vedic period, mantra yoga is the most effective of all of them. Even if another discipline of yoga is followed, for example, *Bhakti* (devotion), *Jnana* (knowledge), *Karma* (selfless action), *Tantra*, etc., chanting of mantra is generally coupled with it, for a catalytic action. And again, although each path is singly sufficient to bring enlightenment, an integrated use of all of them is recommended for quick and safe results. Thus mantra yoga is the most effective one and it is unavoidable, even if another discipline is being followed. Chanting of mantra pulls the *atman* out of worldly pursuits and unites the 'lower self' with the 'higher self'.

There are four ways of chanting a mantra: *Vaikhari Japa* — chanting loudly, *Upamsu Japa* — whispering or humming, *Manasika Japa* — chanting mentally, and *Likhita Japa* — writing the mantra. One has to begin with the Vaikhari Japa, but after some time, when the self-generating forces come into being, the Manasika Japa takes over by itself, and then the mantra is more effective. Those who like to write down the mantra can use the Likhita Japa. The results of all the Japas are more or less the same. Chanting attunes the practitioner to the divine melody which brings harmony to the body and mind. Finally, Cosmic and Supra-cosmic consciousness are released, and the practitioner receives illumination and immortality. As mentioned earlier, you get linked up with the chain of Gurus who attained realisation through the same mantra, and eventually you also become a member of the same chain.

It is good to set a goal or clarify your ideals before starting. Once you have become involved in the process, there may be several excuses to discontinue chanting, which should be overcome with firm determination. There are *asanas,* such as *vajrasana,* which help the practitioner to concentrate and overcome distraction. I always recommend and advise my students to select *hatha yoga* practices because of their two-fold advantage —

ensuring mental concentration, and achieving a healthy body. There is a special charm in developing your personality in all its aspects — physical, mental, emotional and spiritual. Look at Lord Rama or Krishna, they were like that. It is good to thank and bow down respectfully to the Gurus who have realised the 'truth' through the same mantra; they are there to help you, as and when required.

Chanting of a mantra should be accompanied by counting the beads of a set of beads called a 'mala'. The beads can be made of ordinary wood, tulsi, rudraksha or sandal-wood, depending on your choice. The mala is made up of 108 beads and a 'bigger bead' is placed where the set is tied up. The bigger bead symbolises God or Self-realisation. You are not supposed to cross the bigger bead; instead you should turn back. This means that we want to stop the chain of reincarnations. The beads are moved between the thumb and the ring finger only. The mala is held at the level of the heart, to remind us that the lower levels are to be transcended. The best time to chant is between 4 and 6 in the morning, between 11.45 and 12.15 in the afternoon, and between 6 and 7 in the evening. This is the time when spiritual forces can be more active in nature; it is called *Brahma Muhurta*. It is advisable to fix the timing, the *asana* (cushion), and the period of chanting. The cushion should be a bad conductor of electricity, and you should not sit with your back touching the wall, so that the power gained through chanting is not lost. Yogis are known to use cushions of tiger or deerskin for this purpose. Other materials can also be used. One can sit in *padmasana, siddhasana* or *sukhasana,* according to one's training or convenience. One can also sit on a chair; I always chanted while sitting on a chair. In any case, the back should be straight, so that the vibrations can smoothly move upwards. This also makes the path of the Kundalini smooth, whenever it is awakened.

Karma yoga makes us free from all desires, *Jnana* yoga gives us the knowledge that there is a divine power, and *Bhakti* yoga manifests the Divine Being as the diety of the mantra we have been chanting. These are the teachings of the *Vedas.*

For all this to happen you should have a picture of the deity of the mantra before you. By worshipping Him, and offering flowers and food regularly with reverence, we begin to develop a personal link with the Divine. We get love, mercy and help from Him. The Image of God that is manifested is the same as the one we have created and nurtured in our minds. It could be Lord Shiva, Lord Krishna, Lord Jesus Christ, Divine Mother or even your own spiritual teacher.

Close your eyes and concentrate between the eyebrows. Be assured that God is listening to you, and that you will get an answer to your prayers. Many people keep some water in a vessel in front of the picture of God, for as long as the period of chanting lasts, which is normally a couple of months. After offering prayers, they take a sip of that water every day. You will be surprised to know that the water remains fresh for the entire period, without any chemical additives or preservatives. Eventually you may feel a Divine Touch, hear an Inner Sound and see an Inner Light, representing God.

Benefits of Mantras

Emotions have great power over human beings. We all know of innumerable people who have harmed humanity due to their uncontrolled emotions. History is full of such instances. Not even love is safe unless it is generously shared with others, which is what the great ones have done. Self-love is destructive and turns back on the person. It is here that mantra comes into the picture. With regular chanting, a mantra begins to purify the practitioner; eliminates the concern, justification and gratification of the 'self', and finally turns powerful emotions towards God, culminating in the realisation of the Self/God. This is an unparalleled benefit of mantra.

It is better if one understands the meaning of mantra, and then meditates on its meaning while chanting; this increases the surety and the speed of attainment of the goal. However, even the mechanical chanting of a mantra brings results because of the inherent *shanti* in it. The speed of attainment may be slower, but achievement of the goal is guaranteed. In Hindu scriptures there is this story about a robber who, after committing various heinous crimes, wanted peace but refused to chant the name of Lord Rama. Someone advised him to repeat the word 'mara', meaning dead, instead. He did not mind doing this, not realising that, in Hindi, mara becomes Rama on being reversed. He chanted mara, mara, mara... intermittently for hours and days; and in continuation the mantra became Rama, Rama, Rama... Hence the robber attained

Self-realisation by chanting the name of Lord Rama in reverse. Such is the power of chanting a mantra, that irrespective of whether you do or do not know the meaning — the desired goal is achieved. I advise people to commence the process without any preparations. The force of their determination will help them in different forms when it is needed. Even the guru appears, at the right time, when the disciple is ready.

Emotions, on purification through chanting of a mantra, become 'true feelings', which are powerful tools in your hands. Negative habits slowly turn into positive ones, with the mantra acting like a shield against the disturbances. Your definition of love and joy will change. Older thought patterns will get revised. Ego is confronted directly and you begin to understand the obstacles in your way. Humility, stillness and an equipoised state will set in, which are necessary for the awakening of the Higher consciousness. The 'over- sensitivity' due to worries, anger, fears or loneliness is turned into a tool which is so necessary for Self-realisation. In such moments of 'over-sensitivity' you should express your true feelings towards God, in the form of an honest prayer, and should continue with the chanting of mantra. If the chanting of mantra is somewhere in the background, then whatever you are doing will become easier and joyful. Eventually you will become aware of an energy flow within you, and one day you will hear the inner Cosmic Sounds. The Kundalini or the Higher Self may then take charge of your affairs.

Methods of Chanting Mantras

When I have breakfast in the morning, I pray as follows: "God almighty, I thank you very much for the nice food. With all my love, I invite you to take it. I invite all the inhabitants of heaven and earth to have this food. Please take it and honour me." I say a similar prayer at lunch and dinner. You can also try this with a childlike reverence and sincere feelings, and see the difference. When you go to a place of worship – a temple, a mosque, a church – one day you may find that you want to cry, and you do cry. Tears will roll out of your eyes uncontrollably, representing joy that you have finally come to your True Home, and also representing sorrow that you took so many life-times to do that. I have seen many of my friends as well as strangers weeping bitterly at such places. Over-whelmed by emotions I sometimes feel like crying before a lecture. These intense feelings may have been triggered by the thoughts of God revolving in my head.

Many people find it difficult to concentrate when they begin to chant a mantra. The best way to concentrate, especially on the Third Eye position, is to regularly practise some selected *hatha yoga* postures. For this I refer you to my book of the same series on *Hatha Yoga*. Another way, with or without hatha yoga, is to fix longer periods for chanting everyday. The best time is the three hours between 3 and 6 in the morning. In the first hour there will be no concentration and you may even feel restless. In the second hour you begin to get concentration and you remember to keep a count of the malas you have completed. In the third hour you will get real concentration and you may even forget to keep a count of the malas. It is in the third hour that you get spiritual experiences. However, the time required for attaining spiritual experiences cannot be specified. It depends on many factors: your preparation from previous lives, the point of evolution you stand at presently, the point of commencement in this life, and the degree of intensity and devotion at present.

To avoid getting bored of chanting, you can make variations, such as, chanting fast sometimes and sometimes slow, sometimes loud and sometimes softly, by laying stress on one word at times and on another at other times, and so on. Since chanting exercises the system within you and draws energy from the cosmos, you will find many favourable changes in yourself. For example, you may be hearing better, you may be seeing better and your voice may become more melodious. Express joy over these improvements. You should surrender your will to the will of God. Christians say 'Thy will be done'. Faith and surrender in English, *raja va tavakkul* in Islam, and *vishwas* and *samarpan* in Hindi are the pillars for getting the grace of God. Pray to God that He should think through your mind, He should taste through your mouth, He should act through your body and so on. You should try to surrender your whole personality to Him with love and faith.

Another important practice is to maintain a spiritual diary, in which you can write all kinds of happenings and experiences.

Dreams are an important window through which you can see your development, and take guidance from time to time. As you evolve, the cosmic energy within changes in four stages: ignorance, sex, love and spiritual experience. This development is reflected in your dreams through the changing forms of anima, a female figure, if you are a male; or of animus, a male figure, if you are a female. Regularly recording your dreams in a diary and reviewing them, can tell you the level of spiritual development you have reached. Examples of characters appearing in dreams at the four levels are:

Cosmic Energy	Anima	Animus
Primitive (ignorance)	Eve	Tarzan
Romantic (sex)	Cleopatra	P. B. Shelley
Loving (love)	Virgin Mary	Lloyd George
Spiritual (spirituality)	Mona Lisa	Mahatma Gandhi

A certain number of repetitions are required for a mantra to bring about the desired results. For example, it may be required that a mantra be repeated 12 lakh (1.2 million) times. You may calculate how many times you are repeating it in 2 or 3 hours, or whatever time you chant daily and then in how many months or years you can complete the required number. The count is fixed roughly as a guide to the practitioner. You may repeat the whole count once again if you feel that the result is not evident. In fact, it is best to fix daily hours for chanting, and then continue chanting for months or years till the results begin to show, which you will know automatically and unfailingly. And then you will know when to stop chanting and pass on to the next discipline or way of living. You may develop a sense of detachment and witness events, without involving yourself; and/or you may experience the materialisation of the deity; and/or your Inner Self or Psychic Being or your Higher Self may begin to talk to you in dreams and direct visions, and so on. Inner happiness, bliss, freedom from fear of death, visits to higher realms, etc., are the added benefits. The Higher Self takes charge of your activities and replaces ego. You will know it when it happens. As the chakras open up, the experiences also keep changing.

Initially you are a spiritual baby, and you grow as the chanting progresses. At a later stage you may get some inner guidance to change the method of chanting, or even to change the mantra to another one, which should be gladly accepted. But make sure that it is through experience and not due to some assumption or ego problem.

God can be known or approached in many different ways. In the path of devotion you can relate to God as your guru, father, mother, brother, sister, son, friend or your beloved, depending on your feelings. People have been known to achieve success through each one of these relations. Nevertheless, relating to God as mother is best because the mother always pardons the child for all his or her mistakes and is ready to give love unconditionally. However, any relation will work, provided it is taken sincerely and with total faith and surrender.

Choosing a Mantra

Meaning and Purpose of Selective Mantras

Knowledge of the meaning of a mantra, coupled with the creative power of the mind keeps you engrossed in chanting, on one hand, and it can make the results come faster, on the other. As we meditate on the meaning, the virtues of mantra begin to enter our body and mind. The result of concentrating on anything is to attract its qualities towards oneself. For example, if you concentrate on the picture of Lord Krishna or meditate on Him mentally while chanting, His virtues will start entering your self. Like Him you will begin to become equipoised, calm, smiling, etc. His latent qualities will also un-knowingly begin to enter your self. Finally, you may begin to look like Him. Similarly, meditating on the meaning of the mantra while chanting or otherwise will automatically transfer its essence into you. We begin with the very first mantra, which, in fact, is the origin of all other mantras, and that is *Aum*, written as *Om* in short.

Aum

It is the first sound which created every other thing in the universe. It is a manifestation of Brahman himself. A… should be chanted from the region of *mooladhara* and should slowly move to the region of *solar plexus,* U… from the region of sternum, and M… starting from the throat and culminating at *ajna* between the eyebrows. Thus we cover all the chakras from *mooladhara* to *ajna,* visualising that the Kundalini is awakening at the 'root centre', and passing through all the chakras before arriving at the 'eyebrow centre', thus opening our Third Eye. The first part of the sound should be prounced as *AH*, the second part as *OO*, and the third part as *MM*. You may also visualise the lotuses in their respective colours as you pass through the chakras. This will facilitate the arousal of Kundalini and opening of the Third Eye, which is the goal of chanting mantras. While chanting *MM* from *ajna* you should concentrate on the reverberating sound. In fact, one should be aware of the complete mantra from the beginning to the end. Awareness is the key to realisation. You may hear many sounds, and finally the unstruck *pranava* or cosmic *Aum* itself.

The trinity of *Aum* covers the whole creation: beginning, middle and end; unconscious, conscious and supra-conscious; waking, dreaming and dreamless sleep; physical, mental and spiritual; creation, sustenance and destruction — Brahma, Vishnu and Mahesh. The flute of Lord Krishna is also taken to represent the primordial sound of *Aum*. The practitioner should be hollow (egoless) like the flute,

should surrender lovingly to the
will of Krishna, should concentrate
on a single note of the flute, and then
one day he or she may actually hear
the real cosmic *Aum*. With the sound
of the flute, the practitioner travels
back to the source, to one's True
Home, to the plane of Krishna.

Gayatri Mantra

Om, Bhuh, Bhuvah, Swah,
Tat Savitur Varenyam,
Bhargo Devasya Dheemahi,
Dhio Yo Nah Prachodayat.

This is, perhaps, the most
important and ancient mantra,
which is capable of liberating the

humans from the bondage of 'maya' (illusion) if chanted with proper understanding of its meaning. This mantra alone is capable of providing Self/God realisation. I present its meaning with its various aspects, in collaboration with Avadh Bihari Lal Gupta of Delhi.

Present Day Meaning

O God! You are omnipresent, omnipotent and omniscient. You are knowledge and bliss. You are the destroyer of fear, and the creator of this universe, and you are the greatest of all. We bow and meditate upon your light. You guide our intellect in the right direction.

Brief History

The great war of Mahabharat, destroyed not only the warriors alone, but also the intelligentsia. Then came the era of invaders, Shakas, Hunas, Muslims and finally Britishers. During this period the intelligentsia was slain and scriptures were burnt. There is evidence to show that there had been planned efforts to manipulate and pollute the original records. Thankfully however, Dara Shikoh, the elder brother of Aurangzeb, did a great service to Hinduism, by getting the *Upanishads* translated into Arabic. From the Arab countries, the *Upanishads* reached the other European countries.

Scientific Background

Our galaxy is called the Milky Way or Akash-Ganga. It consists of approximately 100,000 million stars. Each star is similar to our Sun, though some are much, much bigger in size. Each star has its own solar system like our Sun and its solar system. There are approximately 10,000 million galaxies like our Milky Way. Many of them are much bigger than our galaxy. We may refer to our galaxy as our universe and all the galaxies put together may be called the cosmos. We know that the moon revolves round the earth and the earth revolves round the Sun, along with the moon. All planets revolve around the Sun. Each of the above bodies rotates on its own axis as well. The Sun, with its planets, revolves round the galactic centre and completes one revolution in 22.5 crore years. All the galaxies in the universe are moving away at a terrific velocity of 20,000 miles per second.

Scientific Meaning

Now step by step we will discuss the scientific meaning of the Gayatri Mantra:

Om Bhuh Bhuvah Swah

Bhuh—The Earth

Bhuvah—The Planets

Swah—The Galaxies (Heaven)

In daily life, when an ordinary fan moves at a speed of 9000 (rpm), it makes noise. Then, imagine what a great noise is produced when the great galaxies move at a speed of 20,000 miles per second. This is what this part of the mantra explains, that the sound produced due to the fast movement of the heavenly bodies is *Om*. This was the sound heard by Rishi Vishwamitra while he was meditating. When he mentioned this to his colleagues, they unanimously decided to call this sound — *Om* meaning the name of God. Because this sound is available in all the three periods of time, hence it is *Sat* (a permanent feature). Therefore, this was the first revolutionary idea to identify formless God with a specific title (form) called *Upadhi*. Until that time, everybody recognised God as formless and nobody was prepared to accept this new idea. In *Gita* also, it is said, 'Omiti Ekaksharam Brahm', meaning, that the name of the supreme is *Om*, which contains only one syllable (8/12).

This sound *Om* heard while in a samadhi was called, by all the Rishis, as *Naad-brahm* (a very great noise), not like pop music. It is normally beyond the specific amplitude prescribed for human hearing. Hence the Rishis called this sound *Udgith* (a musical sound from the heavens above). They also noticed that the infinite mass of galaxies moving with a velocity of 20,000 miles per second was generating a kinetic energy ($\frac{1}{2}mv^2$) and this was balancing the total energy consumption of the cosmos. Hence they named this *pranavah*, which means the body (*vapu*) or the storehouse of energy (*prana*).

To locate any person, we require at least two things:

- Name
- Form

After the identification of the name, the other identification was located by Rishis, as the Light, since it is abundantly available in all the innumerable stars. This is indicated below:

Tat Savitur Varenyam

Tat — That God,

Savitur — The Sun (Star),

Varenyam — Worthy of Respect.

Once we know the form of a person along with the name, we may locate the person. Hence the two titles *(upadhis)* provide the base for identifying the formless God, as Vishwamitra suggested. He told us, that we could know (realise) unknowable, formless God through the known factors, viz., *Om* and the light of the stars.

Bhargo Devasya Dheemahi

Bhargo — The Light,

Devasya — Of the deity,

Dheemahi — We should meditate.

The Rishis instruct us to meditate upon the available forms (light of the stars) to discover the formless creator (God). Also they want us to do *japa* (chanting) of the word *Om* (This is understood in the Mantra). This is how Rishis want us to proceed, but there is a great problem in reaching the state of realisation. The human mind is so restless, that without the grace of the Supreme (Brahm) the mind cannot come to rest. Hence, the Rishis advise us to pray to Him as mentioned below:

Dhio Yo Nah Prachodayat

Dhio — Intellect,

Yo — Who,

Nah — We all,

Prachodayat — Guide to right direction.

It means 'O God! Deploy our intellect on the right path'.

Complete Scientific Interpretation

- Since the earth *(Bhuh)*, the planets *(Bhuvah)* and the galaxies *(Swah)* are moving at a very great velocity, the sound *Om* (the name of formless God) is produced.

- That God *(Tat)*, who manifests Himself in the form of the light of the stars *(Savitur)* is worthy of respect *(Varenyam)*.

- We all, therefore, should meditate *(Dheemahi)* upon the light *(Bhargo)* of the deity *(Devasya)* and should also do *japa* (chanting of *Om*).

- May He *(Yo)* guide our *(Nah)* intellect *(Dhio)* in the right direction *(Prachodayat)*.

So we notice, that the important points researched into by Rishi Vishwamitra and hinted in the mantra are:

- Realising the importance of the syllable *Om*, other religions adopted this word with slight changes eg., *Amen* and *Ameen*.

- God could be realised through the *saguna upasana* (gross method), viz:

  — by chanting the name of the Supreme as *Om*.

  — by meditating upon the light emitted by the stars.

It appears that hereafter the icons of various deities were designed with radiance (aura) around their heads. *Puranas* were written in the language of symbols and stories, to convey the knowledge of Upanishadic wisdom, beautifully and palatably, to the common masses. Similarly, in the world of Psychics, Einstein derived the formula, $E = mc^2$, and the technology to evolve nuclear energy followed.

Any new idea is normally met with opposition, and so the followers of the formless God did not easily agree to accept this new idea. Ultimately, Rishi Vishwamitra won the war and Rishi Vashisht agreed to award the title of *Brahmrishi* to Rishi Vishwamitra as a valued recognition of his great research. This meant, that ultimately, the method of realising formless God through titles (*upadhis*) and symbols was recognised. This method formed a firm basis for the *Vedas* and *saguna upasana*, and this is why the *Gayatri Mantra* has been termed as the mother of *Vedas (Ved Mata)*. Perhaps inspired by this recognition, the Rishi of the *Kathopanishad* also advised that we meditate upon a thumb-sized light that emits no smoke, as a symbol of *Atman*. He states, *Angusth Matra Purusho*

Jyotiriva Dhumka (section IV/13). It appears, that thereafter twelve *Jyotirlingas* were constructed at selected sites in the country as the base for *saguna upasana*. That is why, Lord Krishna in *Gita* (chapter 12, shloka 2) told Arjun to worship the Lord preferably in the *saguna* form instead of the formless *nirguna*, because it is simpler to practise.

The Traditional Meaning

In the traditional meaning qualitative phrases like O God! You are the Creator, giver of knowledge, all light and bliss, remover of fear and so on, have been used. The ultimate result of this is also the same, that is, the practitioner reaches godhood by perpetually meditating upon the meanings of these qualitative phrases. Thus, *Gayatri Mantra*, that derives its greatness from the scientific meaning, was named Prayer Mantra, as not many students could understand the scientific interpretation discussed in the previous paragraphs. Hence, the traditional meaning now available to us became popular and the public, not knowing the Sanskrit and having no knowledge of Astrophysics, accepted this meaning out of *Shradha* (reverence).

Om Mani Padme Hum
This is another very powerful and ancient mantra of Tantric Buddhism, especially popular in Tibet, and is supposed to be related to the Chinese Goddess Kwan Yin. The sound of *Om* induces enlightenment and the literal meaning of the words *mani padme* is jewel in the lotus or *lingam* in the *yoni*, that is the male organ within the female organ. It signifies the wisdom that generates energy and represents the complete state of

wholeness. *Hum* is pronounced as 'hoom' and the sound carries the power to force the mantra into realisation. Tantric Buddhists carry a special kind of two-pronged staff called *vajra*, which symbolises the energy of mantra. One who holds the *vajra*, carries the energy and is called *vajrapani*.

The sound of *hum* is produced by gently and continuously rubbing the rim of a bell with a stick. This sound is sustained for as long as one is engaged in meditation. The sound so produced is supposed to represent the sound of *Om* in practice, to induce enlightenment. It is the culmination of the unification of sexual energy, yoga and the chanting of mantra. One has to concentrate on harmonising the sound with the chanting of the mantra and send the vibrations up the spine to the crown centre. When the dormant energy at the root of the spine awakens, and rises to the crown centre, bliss is experienced, knowledge is intuited and enlightenment results.

To put it simply, chant the mantra silently as you inhale, and chant it audibly, syllable by syllable as you exhale. With some practice a rhythm will be formed, which may be different for different individuals. You should practise the mantra daily for a fixed period of time and should continue practising for months and years, till enlightenment results. The mantra is known to have latent *shakti* in it, and in whatever way it may be chanted, enlightenment is supposed to be the final outcome. However, its potency is of the highest order when male and female principles are in perfect combination, representing the condition of enlightenment.

Comments

The above mantras have been time-tested for the sole purpose of liberation from the bondage of *maya* or illusion and for achieving enlightenment. There is no desire to demand anything from God. Then there are mantras, which help in achieving specific goals. In this category I will give details of the mantras according to their utility. Later some more mantras have been given, that are used to achieve smaller goals in life.

I recommend the trinity of three mantras for the three representative

Gods: (i) Lord Ganesh or the Elephant God before starting anything, for general success, (ii) Lord Shiva for longevity, and freedom from disease and accidents, and (iii) Lord Krishna for family and worldly happiness on the one hand and liberation from *maya* on the other, finally guiding the soul to His abode. Beautiful pictures of Lord Ganesh, Lord Shiva and Lord Krishna should be placed in a room. Fresh flowers should be offered to them every morning. Some incense of your choice will make the atmosphere nicer. Care should be that shoes, drinks, cigarettes, 'e not brought into the room, for you are going to develop a personal relationship with God.

The details of the mantras are as follows:

Lord Ganesh — Siddhi Vinayaka Mantra

Om Namo Siddhivinayaka
Sarvakaryakartre Sarvavighna
Prashamanaya Sarvarajya
Vashyakarnaya Sarvajan Sarvastree
Purushakarshanaya Shreeng Om
Swaha.

The literal meaning of the mantra is that, I bow down to *Siddhivinayaka* (Lord Ganesh), the giver of success, the doer of all works, the remover of all obstacles, the giver of control, making one the most attractive of all men and women. I worship and surrender to Him. The chanting of this mantra provides success in all undertakings, and everyone you encounter behaves humbly and is helpful to you. Chanting of one *mala* every morning provides all the benefits described above.

If this mantra is chanted before chanting any other mantra, the other mantras become more effective. The best time for chanting this mantra is between 12 noon and 2 p.m. You should try this for a period of 2 months at least before expecting any results. If you feel that success has not been achieved, you should chant it for another two months. The 'pundits' have prescribed many formalities for chanting of mantras, which I do not find practical or necessary. The sheer force of your faith, devotion and determination will make the mantra effective. Another method suggested is to sacrifice 10 per cent of your chanting in the holy fire. This requirement can be easily met by chanting 10 per cent of the mantra again. There are many other advantages of this mantra, similar to the ones described on the awakening of the 'root chakra' or *mooladhara*. This is so because Lord Ganesh is the presiding deity of mooladhara.

Lord Shiva — Maha Mrityunjaya Mantra

Om Hraun Om Joong Saha Bhurbhuvaha Swaha Trayambakama Yajamahe Sugandhim Pushtivardhanama Urva Rukmiv Bandhanana Mratyormukshiya

Mamratata Bhurbhuvaha Swarong Joong Saha.

This mantra is said to be the most loving mantra of Lord Shiva. For removing the fear of death and to attain fearlessness from untimely death in any form, this mantra is more potent than any other mantra. This mantra has tremendous power to conquer disease, and to provide a beautiful and healthy body until the last day on earth. The practitioner commands respect and reverence in society, achieves long life, and his dependants are also secured against bad health, disease and untimely death. The mantra should be repeated every day for 1 to 3 hours; depending on how much time you wish to set aside for it, and whether you have other mantras also to be chanted within the available time. The prescribed number of times the mantra should be repeated is 125 thousand, and 10 per cent is required to be sacrificed in the holy fire. The sacrifice can be replaced by chanting the 10 per cent again.

Lord Shiva is in charge of destruction, but He is the simplest of all the deities, and can be pleased easily. The practitioner should pray

Him with complete faith and rrender in order to destroy one's attachment to power, position, worldly possessions and relations, and to get released from the bondage of *maya* or illusion. You have to pay this price to reach the Higher Realm.

Lord Krishna — Gopal Mantra

Kleeng Krishnaya Govindaya Gopijan Vallabhaya Swaha.

This mantra attracts the qualities of Lord Krishna towards the practitioner. It provides all kinds of pleasures and comforts in life, and the soul is merged with Krishna in the end. Thus, this is the best mantra for attainting family and worldly happiness on one hand, and achieving the Kingdom of God on the other. The practitioner should cry for the love of Krishna like a child cries for his/her parents. Krishna is also the Cosmic Lover, and one should crave for His love as Meera Bai did, and achieved her goal with overwhelming success. Meera Bai said that all souls on earth are females and Lord Krishna is the only male. Ramakrishna Paramahansa perhaps believed in this and loved Krishna in this manner. It is said that he developed breasts and he even started to menstruate towards the last days of his practice. This was an exceptional case. Sri Aurobindo was blessed with the vision of Krishna and many others have done so. I saw him as *Bal Krishna* more than once. We cannot command Him to appear before us, but whenever we have qualified for it, He appears before us in our most unexpected moments.

The prescribed number of repetitions for the mantra is 1100 thousand, and 10 per cent is to be sacrificed in the holy fire. However,

I would advise you not to restrict
yourself to any limit, and to
continue with the chanting until you
know that you have attained your
goal.

Comments

The above three Mantras are very
potent and have been tested by
many practitioners. I would
recommend that you divide the
daily chanting time equally between
the three mantras, or take only one
of them, according to your
requirement or choice. You may first
experience the death of ego, then
resurrection and then have the

ion of your chosen deity one day
the process. You might have
started chanting for a specific goal.
But at a particular juncture you may
not have the same desire for that
worldly goal anymore. After seeing
the beauty of the Higher Realm,
even though for a very short period,
the whole outlook of the
practitioner changes. You become
peaceful, desireless, and radiate
love unconditionally.

Other Mantras

Om Namo Bhagawate Vasudevaya
A powerful mantra of Lord Vishnu.
The practitioner does not want to

achieve any earthly goal, and prays to bow down to God who pervades every particle of the Universe around him or her. A minimum of 10 malas, must be chanted every day, till the realisation of the goal. However, the prescribed number of repetitions for chanting of the mantra is 1200,000 times, with 10 per cent to be sacrificed in the fire.

Om Namaha Shivaya
Although a shorter mantra of Lord Shiva, as compared to the former one, it is very effective. It is specially for the householders who do not have much time to devote and

cannot observe the associated formalities. The practitioner has no desire for wordly pleasures, and chanting of this mantra is supposed to bring enlightenment, along with the vision of Lord Shiva. A minimum of 10 malas must be chanted everyday. The prescribed number of repetitions is 1000,000 times.

Om Namo Narayanaya
This is another mantra of Lord Vishnu. It is simple and very useful for householders. It should be repeated 500,000 times at least. It brings happiness in the family, unity

and love between the members, attainment of worldly possessions, association with saints and popularity in the society.

Om Ghranih Surya Aditya
This mantra offers prayers to the Sun God and attracts the virtues of the Sun. It is especially designed to eradicate the inherent defects of vision and to improve the power of the eyes. In addition to that, the face of the practitioner becomes brighter and success is achieved in general matters of life. It improves the memory, and the practitioner attains worldwide acclaim. Good health,

...g life and physical possessions
...e the other associated benefits.

*Om Ganesh Rinam Chhingi Varenyam
Hung Namaha Phat*
This mantra is especially designed
for those who are suffering due to
monetary problems. Regular
chanting of this mantra removes
poverty from the house and makes
the individual self-sufficient.

*Om Namo Bhagawate Varaha Rupaya
Bhurbhuvaha Swaha, Satyapte Bhupati-
tvam Dehyate Dadapaya Swaha*
This mantra is specially designed
for those who are involved in
fighting, to provide safety for them

and guarantee their victory over the enemy. It has to be chanted 125,000 times for success.

Ham Hanumate
Rudratmkaya Hung Phat
This mantra has been praised in the scriptures. It is said that Lord Shiva gave it to Lord Krishna, who passed it on to his best friend Arjun who was involved in the great war of Mahabharata. Arjun was victorious and he was universally praised for his heroic acts. It is to be chanted in a lonely place 100,000 times. During the period of chanting, the practitioner should observe

celibacy. A lamp lit with mustard oil should be placed before the picture of Sri Hanuman. On successful completion, the practitioner achieves victory over the enemy and all his physical demands are fulfilled.

Om Namo Harimarkat Markataya
Amukam Harimarkat
Markataya Swaha

This mantra is specially designed to get rid of a person who may be troubling you. Replace the word 'Amukam' by the name of the person who is troubling you and chant the mantra 100,000 times

before the statue of Sri Hanuma[ ]
is believed that the person wh[ ]
against you will himself face the
trouble, and leave your path clear,
on completion of the assigned
number of chantings.

Kleeng Kamdevaya Namaha
Kamdev is the name of the god of
sexual energy. This mantra is
designed for people who want to
acquire enough sexual power so as
to satisfy their partners. On
completion of the required number
of chantings, the practitioner is
supposed to acquire a handsome
and healthy physical body. He or

she also acquires the power to attract the opposite sex. The prescribed number of chantings is 300,000. If this mantra fails to work, one can chant the following mantra:

Om Kamdevaya Vidmahe Pushpvanaya Dhimahi Tatno Anang Prachodayat

One is likely to achieve enough sexual energy if this mantra is chanted for one cycle of the mala, every day. One can stop the repetitive chanting after achieving the desired results. This mantra is called 'Kam Gayatri Mantra' and is supposed to be quite powerful.

Saum Somaya Namaha

This mantra is related to the Moon god and is designed for those people who want special respect in society or government adminis-tration. On chanting this mantra 100,000 times, one gets the desired result, which also includes a disease-free body and a long life.

Om Brang Brahaspataye Namaha

This mantra is related to Guru Brihaspati or Jupiter. It is effective in providing a child to a woman who is unable to become a mother. It requires 100,000 repetitions.

Om Devaki Sut Govind Vasudev Jagatpate, Dehi Me Tanayam Krishna Tvamaham Sharanam Gataha

The text says that this mantra is quite effective in bringing pregnancy to a woman and getting her a son. A repetition of 100,000 times is required for success. The whole thing can be repeated if required.

Om Vastram Me Dehi Shukraya Swaha

This mantra is related to the god Venus. It is designed to provide all kinds of physical comforts to the practi-tioners. It should be chanted a 100,000 times.

Om Hreeng Dung Durgayai Namaha
This mantra is related to Goddess Durga. It requires a chanting of 100,000 times. It is a powerful mantra for providing a son, victory over enemies, eradication of some diseases and other kinds of physical attainments. The mantra also bestows the power of speech on the practitioner.

Vad Vad Vagvadini Swaha
This mantra is related to Saraswati, the goddess of learning and knowledge. Celibacy and 10,00,000 repetitions are recommended. The practitioner achieves brilliancy in

the field of knowledge and becomes well-known. The following mantra is more powerful:

Om Hreeng Shreeng Aing Vagvadini Bhagawati Arhanmukh Nivasini Saraswati Mamasye Prakasham Kuru Kuru Swaha

The night of Deepawali (festival of lights) is the auspicious time for the chanting of this mantra, when the forces of the goddess of knowledge are naturally awake. The practitioner should wear white clothes, sit facing East and chant the mantra 12,000 times. The mantra is known to attract the ray of the god representing learning and knowledge, and the chanting opens up the corresponding faculty in the brain. Obstacles on the way to learning and acquiring knowledge are eradicated, and the practitioner achieves brilliancy. Students and seekers of knowledge in any field of life can practise this Mantra.

Om Aing Hreeng Kleeng
Chamundaye Vichche

This is the well-known *Navarn Mantra* of 'devi' or goddess, the creative female counterpart of God. It is known to be very powerful and effective. Whenever in difficulty, the practitioner can chant this mantra with faith and devotion, and the situation would be eased soon. A regular practice can pave the way for higher achievements. If the mantra does not suit you, you would know it within a few days and then you can discontinue and look for other alternatives. Variations of this mantra, for pleasing or attracting a particular person towards you are given next.

Om Kleeng Kleeng Om Aing Hreeng Kleeng Chamundaye Vichche 'Amukam' Kleeng Kleeng Mohanam Kuru Kuru Kleeng Kleeng Swaha

Replace the word 'Amukam' in the mantra by the name of the person in your mind and chant the mantra till success is achieved. The person in question will be seen to have changed his or her attitude favourably towards you.

Comments

There are several mathematical formulae for calculating and knowing whether a particular mantra is suitable for the practitioner or not. I would not recommend going in for such calculations. Instead I would suggest that you select a mantra according to your requirements. Within a few days you will know by the effects of chanting whether it is suitable for you or not. If a particular mantra is not suitable, you can try another. Before beginning with chanting, sincerely pray to God for help, and you are bound to get directions from Him.

Using mantras for achieving worldly goals is not the real purpose of this book. Yet, some mantras are presented here for those who only want the satisfaction of certain earthly desires. The main purpose is to get liberation from *maya* or illusion and enter the Kingdom of God. To help you to achieve the goal, some ancient and powerful mantras have been mentioned here and some related facts are also discussed in the following chapters.

Guru for Mantras

A person, who has walked on the spiritual path himself or herself and has achieved the power of mantra, is a guru. Such a person gets an indication from either one's 'physical guru' or 'inner guru', and then he or she is qualified to have disciples. Inner guru is one's own 'psychic being' or 'higher self', a personality developed after many lifetimes. This inner guru is a mediator between the soul of the practitioner and Super soul or God, and it is this agent that brings Self-realisation or God-realisation. The role of the physical guru is to connect the disciple with one's inner guru. Once this is done, the role of the physical guru is over and then the inner guru takes over to guide the disciple, from time to time. From this stage the disciple or the practitioner becomes independent.

There are two kinds of marriages: one is the physical marriage between a man and a woman in the traditional way, the other is the spiritual marriage between the guru and the disciple, when the former gives initiation to the latter. Just as in a physical marriage, you have strong vows and obligations in the spiritual marriage also. The guru takes the responsibility of helping the disciple to attain Self-realisation. The former in many cases has to take the load of *karmas* of the latter, for his or her progress. The guru has to see the possible ways in which the disciple can make progress, and he may suggest certain ways of living and doing things, which may be different from the disciple's usual routine. The disciple, similarly, has to take a vow to obey his or her teacher, without questioning, and to serve the guru to the best of his or her capacity. It is a question of faith and surrender. Therefore, the two have to choose each other very carefully. Once it has been done, they are both bound to each other by their vows.

Having a guru is not necessary, but is better in the long run. If one has a guru, it helps in two ways; firstly, the guru knows the way, since he or she has traversed the path himself or herself, and, secondly, he or she infuses the power of mantra into the disciple.

This is like the student being directly admitted to the high school, without passing through the years of primary schooling. However, there have been, and are even today, many brave ones who, for one reason or the other, took the journey alone without a guide, and they got help on the way from nature in many different ways. The guru comes to help such people himself or herself, whenever necessary. In many cases, such travellers find connection with their inner guru themselves, sometimes helped by the invisible helpers. However, in normal cases, it is beneficial to have a guru, if you can find one.

Before taking initiation or *diksha* it is advisable that the disciple gets rid of his or her negative habits, once and for all. If this is not done, progress may be hindered and there is also a chance of a relapse, which can be very dangerous. One should be honest in telling the truth about oneself to the guru, who can decide whether the person is ready for the initiation or not. After this, the person should ensure two things — firstly, that he or she will obey the guru without questioning him, and secondly, that he or she would pursue the path till the end, whatever number of years it may take. Sometimes the guru initiates to clear all the karmas in this lifetime, and the spiritual journey begins only in the next life. For example, a person may be determined to go on a spiritual journey, but he or she may still be having attraction for certain kinds of food or drinks, for mating with the opposite sex, or doing some other thing. Only when there is no desire for wordly pleasures, is one ready for initiation.

fall on a path where the birds can eat it up, or it may fall on the rocky ground where the roots cannot settle down, or it may fall among thorns where it can be destroyed, or it may fall on fertile ground where it can grow and bear fruits. I need not say that He referred to mantra or to the power of mantra when He talked about the seed. Hence the mantra bears fruits only when the right disciple chants it. The initiation consists of three stages. In the first stage, the practitioner is introduced to the mantra. In the second stage he or she is introduced to *brahmacharya* or 'vow of celibacy'. In the third stage the practitioner is introduced to *sanyasa* or renunciation. The periods of time between any two initiations vary, depending on how fast you study the related subject matter, and how soon you can translate the things learnt into practice. In the end one becomes a swami when he or she has qualified to teach the Holy Scriptures.

Next comes the question of finding or choosing the right guru. A real guru has witnessed the *Atman* or Self and he can talk freely about it. He can answer your questions and can also clear all your doubts. He has knowledge of the scriptures and does not differentiate between various religions, faiths or traditions. He has equanimity and balance of mind. He has conquered the five enemies — greed, lust, anger, attachment and ego, which you can easily judge in your talks with him or her. You feel peaceful and experience an elevation of mind when you are in his or her presence. The very thought of money is against spiritual progress. You will find that a real guru is not interested in money matters; he or she will be satisfied with whatever meagre resources are available. A guru has no interest in establishing a new sect, rather the idea is to put knowledge in one place as a pool, wherefrom any one can be benefited. He or she might pioneer an institute of spiritual learning to provide guidance to others. Many, however, do not like to make an ashram and have disciples, and do not like to teach the principles of spirituality as such. Yet, they are known to the world in one way or the other.

It may not always be possible to find a real guru to your satisfaction. I know about late Dr. B.S.Goel, author of *Third Eye and Kundalini* who spent several years in search of a guru. He repeatedly met with failure and was highly dejected. He even went to Puttaparthi three times and saw Sai Baba, who also ignored him. Finally he sat down and devoted himself to genuine efforts. And one night Sai Baba appeared before him in a vision and talked with him. So, if you cannot find a suitable guru, there is no reason for you to be disappointed. You may certainly be knowing someone who has traversed the spiritual path for several years and may have lectured or written books, or may be otherwise known for his work in this field. If you find him honest, if he does not prescribe a fee for what he can give you, if he is devoid of the five enemies — greed, lust, anger, attachment and ego to a good extent, if he can talk about the reality of *Atman* and scriptures, if you find *shanti* (peace) and the answers to most of your questions while talking to him, you can safely start your spiritual journey under his guidance. If you are sincere, and if destiny wants you to be connected to some other person as guru, then that guru will himself appear before you one day. There is no doubt about it. In the absence of finding such a person, select any mantra of your choice and start chanting seriously according to the guidelines presented in this book. Have faith and surrender to God, and Self-realisation will come to you one day. It is a matter of starting; help begins to come in unexpected ways, I can assure you of that.

Other Aspects of Mantras

Healing

Mantras have tremendous healing power. Chanting of a mantra releases the emotions and brings a state of calmness and deep relaxation in the practitioner as well as in the minds of others listening to it. This creates a channel for the spiritual energy flowing through you. Fill your heart with love and compassion and forgive everyone unconditionally. The person to be treated should have faith in God.

Invoke the image of the deity of your choice and visualise the person you want to help engulfed in the Cosmic White Light. Visualise that the person so wrapped in Light is moving towards the deity, the source of the healing Light. Now chant the mantra continuously and visualise that God's healing power and your compassionate love is flowing through your open heart to the person. Some people may feel that the energy flows through their fingertips. In that case it is advisable to put the fingers directly above the person sitting or lying in front of you.

The person may be healed immediately or after some time, or he or she may not be healed at all. Remember the myth that if Jesus healed ten people, only seven of them were cured. This depends on individual karmas and faith. You cannot balance the karmas of others so easily. If the person at the receptive end, has faith, then only will he or she be cured. A powerful yogi may even think of taking the disciple's karmas on himself or herself.

Thoughts are very powerful, beyond one's imagination. They can create and destroy worlds. If one continuously thinks that he or she is a failure, and believes that he or she will be failing in the enterprises undertaken, it will happen just so. If one is positive and optimistic, and believes that his or her involvements will be successful, within the limit of possibilities, then the end result would be positive. If one regularly chants the mantra, 'Aham Brahmasmi' or 'I Am That I Am', then one will realise one's divinity one day. In that case, the person will achieve perfect disease-free health, a spiritually conscious mind and oneness with the Absolute. One last thing I can say is that the attitude of 'letting go' and 'unconditional forgiving of yourself and all others' has the tremendous power of attracting the mercy and grace of God. Make sure that you are not hurting anyone directly or indirectly and not punishing yourself for the pain caused to someone. No one is too great a sinner to be pardoned and healed. Give up all sorts of dependence and become vulnerable and helpless, and you will see that God enters your being, because you have cleared yourself of all the debris.

Proper use

Mantra is a powerful tool of yoga —
connecting the soul with the Super
soul. It should not be used for
worldly achievements, eg, power,
position, possessions, etc. It is the
gateway to revelation and
liberation, and the knowledge
acquired is not lost with physical
death, it carries over to the next
incarnation. And then you start your
journey from a higher level than the
previous incarnation. As the
chanting goes on at the back of the
mind, the power of mantra will
always bring your attention to the

right cause, that is, knowing God. And all those great ones who achieved liberation through this mantra before you will be available for help, as and when required. The whole lineage will be at your disposal, and when your time comes, you will be the new link to the chain. Make it a habit to chant mantra all the time, whether you are relaxing at home or working in office or playing games in the sports centre or buying groceries in the market. And then it would be repeating itself even when you are sleeping. Never give up, till the results are achieved.

Faith is the best way of receiving the grace of God. I will narrate two small stories to illustrate this fact. There was a poor family consisting of a mother and her son living in a village. The child had to pass through a jungle on his way to school every day. Once there was a function in the evening, and every child was to be accompanied by his or her caretaker. This poor child, being afraid of the dark, asked his mother to provide him with a servant to accompany him on the way. The mother had no means for that, but she told the boy that his brother Krishna lived in the nearby jungle and he could call him whenever in trouble. That evening the boy was really scared and sincerely cried for Krishna, since he believed his mother. Lord Krishna appeared and offered His finger to the boy to hold and led him through the jungle. On the way He gave him a small glass of milk as his contribution to the school function, as every child had to bring some item of food.

While the function was going on, the boy presented the small glass of milk as his contribution. Everybody laughed at his humble offering. After a while, someone came running from the kitchen and said that the milk just would not finish in the boy's glass and that all the containers were full. Everyone was surprised. They thought the boy was an extraordinary person. They asked him where he had got that glass from. The boy pointed his finger towards Lord Krishna who was standing there and smiling, and told people that it was He who had escorted him to school all the way. The people were highly surprised, since they could not see the Lord in spite of their lifelong efforts and devotion to God. They asked the boy to show them Lord Krishna. Krishna told the boy that this was not possible, since there was no one qualified enough to see Him. And in the presence of everyone, the boy returned home holding the finger of the Lord, while everyone else kept looking into emptiness.

In another case, a simple man approached a pundit and asked him how to please God. In the eyes of the pundit this uneducated person had no value. He just gave him a small statue of Krishna and told him that it was God. The simple man believed the pundit and took the statue home. He cooked some food and sat down to eat it with God. He talked to the statue in all possible humble ways and offered the food. There was no mantra and no sophisticated way of praying or worshipping. When the simple man saw that God was not eating, he thought that some thing was wrong with him, since the pundit could not have lied. He had great faith in God. When he got tired, he also slept without eating anything. The next day he cooked fresh food and again tried in the same way to make God eat, so that he could also eat. On the second day also, he was not successful.

He tried this for several days and every night he slept hungry, since God would not eat. He became very weak and it was perhaps the last day he could cook. When this time also he was not successful, he said to the statue that now he would neither cook nor do any other thing, since there was no purpose of his living when he could not please God. Just as he was preparing to lie down to die, God materialised through the statue and held the hand of the simple man. All the weakness of the man suddenly disappeared, and both of them ate food and talked about things of common interest. It is said that every night, Krishna would materialise and the two would eat together. When others heard about this happening, they also came to see the Lord and some even tried the same formula themselves. No one was successful and yet, people saw the simple man eating and talking with nothingness. His business prospered and soon he became rich.

Such is the power of faith and real devotion. You do not need any mantra or rituals. The 'truth' is simple but we are complicated. We look for special mantras, methods and gurus to find God, but what we need is 'faith and surrender'. We do not believe in the power of mantra given to us and it is this 'disbelief' which hinders success. Ordinary people who have no spiritual experiences begin to judge their guru immediately. Jnana and spirituality are inner things, which cannot be measured by any physical yardstick. People misunderstand the guru due to his external appearance and way of living. Many a time you come across the real person but you cannot recognise him or her, because you have not earned the grace of God yet. You might have found the philosopher's stone already, and thrown it away, believing it to be an ordinary stone. When the right time comes, whatever mantra and guru you follow, it is the one that is meant to give you Self/God realisation.

Disciples these days are also not easily available to the gurus; in fact, it is easy to find a guru but it is difficult to find a *chela* (disciple). The reason is that young practitioners are arrogant and self-assertive and they do not care for the orders of a guru. They are self-sufficient and independent from the beginning. Buddha worked on the principle of *Neti-Neti* (not this-not this) in the right manner and found God. But these aspirants of the present times have a perverted intellect, and they use the principle of *Neti-Neti* in a wrong and absurd manner. Let us take an example from nature. Heat flows from the higher temperature to the lower one, water flows from higher hydrostatic pressure to the lower one, a ball rolls from a higher gradient to a lower one and so on. Even so, jnana (knowledge) flows from the higher potential to a lower one. That is, only if a learner keeps himself or herself at a lower level than the Guru, in a receptive manner and without ego, then he or she can learn something. Firstly, the ignorant aspirants judge the spiritual depth of the guru with their limited knowledge; secondly, they want the guru to teach them the way they want. They will criticise the guru in one way or the other and will surrender themselves to him in a half-hearted manner. They will not have faith in the mantra given by the Guru and will keep looking for an alternative mantra or an alternative guru. As a result they remain unsuccessful; neither do they get *maya* (world), nor no do they reach Rama (God).

Not only from our Academy of Yoga, but I have information from several contemporary guides and yoga centres in India and abroad, that it is rare to find devoted disciples. People want quick results without dedicating themselves to the process for sufficient time. Even a period of five years is too much for them. To them I say that you need five years of rigorous hard work to get a degree in engineering, medicine or accountancy. Is God cheaper than a degree? A part-time approach to God brings only part-time results. Only a full-time approach can bring full-time results. In our circle I have been hearing from early childhood that you need seven lifetimes to have interest in some guru, seven lifetimes to know about a real guru, and seven lifetimes to be in the guidance of a real guru, before you may know about God. Some of these sayings may appear to be exaggerations, but the meaning conveyed is not difficult to understand. You must sincerely pray to God, day and night, to find a real guru and request Him to show some signs for recognising such a person. For example, the guru may be wearing a particular kind of dress, holding a particular flower or having some other qualifying marks.

Gurus test aspirants in many different ways before accepting them as disciples. Many disciples run away in such a period. They misunderstand the guru and lose their faith in him. In earlier times the aspirants used to clean the ashram, wash clothes, cook food, tend the cows, bring fuel from the jungle, press the guru's body and legs, and so on. These days people consider such acts to be menial. But people these days are unable to perform simple tasks too. For example, an educated aspirant may be asked to do public relations work, arrange material for yoga practices and/or for prayers, attend telephone calls for a few hours a day, serve as a librarian for a few hours a day, and so on. These are not personal duties for the guru, but the disciples find it too much to do. Differences between the aspirants may develop, each may accuse the guru of favouring the other, and these kinds of situations may create another headache for the guru. He may have to forget about giving lessons on spirituality for sometime, to try and come out of such situations.

Many of you may have heard about the great yogi Milarepa of Tibet. He reached that exalted position after devoting half his life to serving a series of gurus with all their whims and fancies. On the other hand we have Swetaketu, who was readily accepted by his guru as a disciple and at the young age of twenty-four, became an expert on *Vedas*. So, different aspirants have to meet with different kinds of situations in life, according to their karma and preparation from previous lives. However, as history tells us, both Milarepa and Swetaketu served their masters in a perfect manner; they did not consider any act as menial. The act of egoless service cleanses the consciousness and prepares the aspirant to be ready to receive something from the guru. Only when there is a real thirst in the practitioner and he or she becomes fit to receive it, does the grace of God come to him or her. However, some of the guidelines for aspirants can be laid down as follows:

Guidelines for Disciples

- The three basic requirements are: truth, non-violence and celibacy. Truth requires you to state facts as they are, under all circumstances. Non-violence requires you to always act in such a way that you do not harm anyone in any manner. As for celibacy, there are some moderations for married practitioners. The crux of the matter in this regard is that one has to preserve one's semen to the maximum. There are yogic disciplines which make you an *urdhvareta* eventually; this means that, the flow of semen is reversed — instead of going down and out, it now goes in and up towards the brain. Indian scriptures describe an *urdhvareta* to be a person *in* the world but not *of* the world; he or she is supposed to have achieved liberation from the cycle of death and rebirth. Try to understand the meaning I wish to convey and set your own boundaries. You have to learn how to reverse its flow.

- Humility, a very important requirement, appears simple but is hard to achieve. By living contented within whatever circumstances you have been put into by nature, having intense aspiration, looking for opportunities to render selfless service to others, having firm faith in guru and God, and by making it a habit to behave equally well under praise and criticism, you can develop 'humility' in due course. Once humility is developed, you are open to the signals from your 'higher self' or God.

- Develop the habit of bearing both insult and injury equally well; crush the ego down to the level that nothing hurts you. An abuse directed at you is only to your name and body in this incarnation. You know that these things will be left behind and only the Soul or *Atman* will pass on to the next world. You must believe in the words of Lord Krishna and Lord Jesus, both of whom laid stress on 'self', which is the real you. If you cannot believe in their words, throw their pictures out of your house. And if you do believe, then do not care about insults and injuries, since they are insignificant. The day you learn this secret, you will witness yourself as 'Atman' or 'Soul', and become free from the bondage of further incarnations on earth.

You will be known as a 'karma yogi' and you will not need a 'guru' or 'mantra', since you will then be at the same level as any enlightened person. Until this thing is not perfectly done, you do need a guru or a mantra. All other virtues mentioned in the texts follow automatically once you have developed 'real humility'. Even many of the so-called gurus do not have real humility.

• Discrimination is another important requirement when you deal with everyday situations in life. It is not so easy to decide about what should be done and what should not be done under any particular circumstances. Most of us say the following words to God in our prayers everyday, "O God, give me the power to like what I have got, and the power to forget what I do not have." In every situation there are two alternatives, and you have to choose one of them. Now how do you do it? You should begin to like what you have and consider things you do not have to be of little use to you.

Have faith in God, He gives you what you need, and will give you, in future, what you do not have if you really need it. If you believe there is God's hand in everything, leave everything in the hands of God. Acting on a situation, discriminate between the one that will do well to others and the one that will do good to only you, and choose the former invariably. If you can do it, you have the power of discrimination. This will lead you to the state of 'desirelessness' which has been talked about by most. It is easy to preach and difficult to achieve. Most of the saints have themselves not reached the state of desirelessness.

- There is only one desire which is free from the bondage of *maya*, and that is to have 'love, faith and surrender to God'. And the one who has this desire gets everything else without efforts. Do you not remember the words of Jesus — "Seek ye the Kingdom of God first, and everything else will be added unto you"?

- Make it a habit to introspect and analyse yourself. Maintain a diary and see what you should have done and what not. If you have to pay a debt to someone in any form, try to find the means to do it. Try to keep your slate clean, so that you can leave this world comfortably whenever He calls you back. If you have not cleaned your slate, this could be the 'seed' to bring you back to earth in another incarnation.

- Never dissuade yourself from the goal of Self/God realisation. By avoiding settling for lesser goals, you can do this. For example, do not wish to become the captain of a team, or to win a match, or to become the director or manager of a firm, or to become the head of a department or superintendent of a section, etc. Whenever such a position comes, accept it as a gift of God and take it as a challenge to perform your duty selflessly. If you are able to do that, you have passed the test, and you are closer to God.

• A guru has a divine nature and a divine way of living and behaving in daily life. You should not be concerned with his way of living, which can be misleading if you begin to analyse with your limited intellect. As an example, the great saint Ramakrishna Paramahansa was an idol of *vairagya* and desirelessness, but he had a great passion for tasteful/delicious food. Once someone sarcastically asked him about it. Ramakrishna smiled and said that he did not expect the question that soon. "However", he said, "since you have asked it, I must reply. This was the only thing which was keeping me on earth, so that I could give you all I had before I leave for good. Now I should leave the food and the world." And within a few days he transmigrated to the Higher realm. Many saints keep a worldly interest alive in themselves so that they should leave their body soon after achieving liberation. This is mainly because they want to complete their teachings due to their love for their fellow beings, and they do not want to leave any seed to come back to earth. Many High Souls like Jesus are knowingly reincarnated on earth to remind human beings of what they have forgotten; but we are not sure whether they were all happy to do it in the end. However, the point is that we should be concerned with the divine nature of the guru and learn from him, rather than looking at his worldly life.

- *Vairagya* or detachment is perhaps not the means but the end of one's existence in the physical world. As Buddha said, attachment is the cause of miseries for human beings. With all the above preparations, detachment may result one day. I would not say that a person should go to the guru after achieving *vairagya*. If he or she has really achieved *vairagya*, which is irreversible, he or she is already on the threshold of union with God. Desire for sensual pleasures is so deep-rooted that it has a fair chance of returning even after its eradication. This has happened to several yogis too. However, when one has tasted the nectar of celestial music and celestial sound through one's inner ears, the chances of reverting are not so high, since one is now in direct communion with the Divine. Yet, caution is necessary. Adherence to sensual pleasures can delay further progress. And detachment is an inner change, not an outer one. You may see hundreds of people on the road in saffron-coloured clothes and shaven head; none of them is perhaps a *vairagi*. They are normally looking for worldly things in saffron garments, which is another way of seeking worldly attainments without labour. A real *vairagi* may be clad in the costliest of suits or in an ordinary dress, may be driving a Mercedes or walking barefoot, eating delicious food or fasting: it is all the same. One whose inner being has been transformed may live in any manner and may do anything externally, he or she would remain *vairagi*. It is a different thing whether you can recognise him or her or not.

Glossary

Ajna — a chakra (energy field) at the eyebrow centre.

Atman — soul

Bal krishna — Lord Krishna in his form as the divine child.

Japa — chanting of a mantra

Jyotirlinga — the twelve holy stones that are believed to have spontaneously emerged from the earth, symbolic of Lord Shiva.

Karmas — actions performed in one's various lifetimes.

Mala — a necklace consisting of 108 beads (the beads can be made of ordinary wood, sandalwood, rudraksha or tulsi, etc.)

Mooldhara — a chakra (energy field) at the root centre.

Pranava — the body storehouse of energy

Nirguna upasana — when the Lord is worshipped as the Formless One.

Saguna upasana — when the Lord is worshipped in a particular form.

Shakti — creative kinetic energy

Vairagi — one who is free from worldly attachments.

Vairagya — detachment